Advanced JMeter
From Load Testing to Performance Engineering

Table of Contents

Chapter 1. Introduction

In an era driven by digitization and rapid technological progress, ensuring software quality, reliability, and efficiency is more important than ever. Our Special Report, "Advanced JMeter: From Load Testing to Performance Engineering," delves into this highly technical but crucially significant sphere. Using detailed, easy-to-follow explanations, the report demystifies advanced concepts of JMeter, effectively guiding professionals to shift from basic load testing to the wider realm of performance engineering. The pivotal role of this report is to empower you to design robust, efficient systems capable of handling unforeseen traffic spikes, thereby enhancing end-user satisfaction. So through this rigorous journey of methodical insights, practical examples, and industry-best tools, let's conquer the pinnacle of system performance together. No matter how steep the learning curve may seem, remember: in a world competing for speed and efficiency, staying ahead is the only way to win.

Chapter 2. Understanding the ABCs of JMeter

JMeter is an open-source software, a 100% pure Java application, designed to load test functional behavior and measure performance. Originally designed for testing web applications, it has since expanded to other test functions.

2.1. Getting Started with JMeter

To get started with JMeter, you must first install it on your computer. JMeter is available for download from the Apache website. It is a portable application, meaning it doesn't need to be installed – you only have to extract the .zip or .tgz file and run the .bat or .sh file inside the 'bin' folder to start JMeter.

2.2. JMeter Interface Breakdown

When you open JMeter, you will be greeted with a user-friendly console. The left panel contains the test plan, and the right panel called 'workbench' is the area where you create and manage your tests. The main elements included in a JMeter interface are ThreadGroup, Controllers, Samplers, Logic Controllers, Listeners, Timers, Assertions, and Config Elements. Understanding these elements is crucial to leverage the power of JMeter effectively.

2.3. Understanding ThreadGroup

A ThreadGroup is a collection of threads. In the JMeter context, each 'thread' represents a user using your application. The 'Thread Group' panel allows you to set the number and sequence of each user request.

2.4. Controllers and Samplers

Controllers in JMeter drive the processing of a test. They are divided into two types: Samplers and Logic Controllers. Samplers allow JMeter to send specific types of requests to a server, fetching 'samples' which are processed by JMeter. These samples could be a HTTP, FTP, JDBC, or any other kind of request.

2.5. Logic Controllers

Logic Controllers dictate the order of processing of samplers in a test. For example, a Loop Controller will tell a Sampler to repeat its request a set number of times, another Logic Controller might randomly choose which Sampler to process, a third might send a Sampler request based on a condition, and so forth.

2.6. JMeter's Listeners

Listeners provide access to the data gathered by JMeter about the test samples. The results can be viewed or saved to a file in several formats including a tree, table, graph or log file. Listeners should be used sparingly as they can eat up a lot of memory if there is a large amount of sample data generated.

2.7. Timers in JMeter

Timers are the JMeter's way of handling the speed at which a test is conducted. They are used to pause between each request which can be crucial for a more accurate simulation of user interaction.

2.8. JMeter Assertions

Assertions are the way JMeter checks the responses from your server word, matching your specifications. Each assertion tests a different aspect of your request - Response Assertions check the server response, Size Assertions confirm the response size, XML Assertions look into XML structure, etc.

2.9. Config Elements

These elements can add or modify requests. They can be used to set up defaults and variables for later use within the test script. They are processed at the start of the scope in which they're found. Some of the Config Elements include HTTP Request Defaults, HTTP Cookie Manager, and User Defined Variables.

2.10. Building Your First Test Plan

A JMeter Test Plan is the overall container for your test scenario. It defines what to test and how to go about it. Building a test plan involves adding the various elements mentioned above and setting their properties. The plan should be clear, easy to navigate, and tied to your testing objectives.

2.11. Advanced Techniques in JMeter

As you become more comfortable with JMeter's basics, there are many advanced techniques that you can learn. These include, but are not limited to: Distributed Testing, Handling User Sessions With URL Rewriting, AJP (Apache JServ Protocol) Sampling, and Using the JDBC Sampler.

In closing, understanding the ABCs of JMeter is a journey beginning with installation, through interface navigation and concepts comprehension, to planning and executing tests, and eventually mastering advanced techniques. The mission may seem daunting, but with a systematic approach, it becomes part of your software performance engineering toolkit, empowering you to deliver robust, efficient systems.

Chapter 3. Transitioning From Testing To Engineering: A Paradigm Shift

Software testing, specifically load testing, is traditionally seen as a silo-ed task done in the latter stages of project workflows. But with the advent of agile methodologies and continuous integration and deployment practices, its role and importance have evolved. We are now transitioning towards the broader area of performance engineering, placing a proactive, comprehensive focus on system performance throughout the development life cycle.

3.1. Understanding the Shift

The shift from load testing to performance engineering is not just about a change in tasks; it's about an alteration in mindset. Load testing typically involves assessing a system under varying loads to determine its response times, throughput rates, and resource utilization levels. While it's a crucial part of evaluating system performance, it's often reactive and applied after the bulk of the development work is completed.

Performance engineering, on the other hand, is a proactive approach, integrated from the initial stages of the project, that factors performance into all aspects of development - design, implementation, testing, and deployment. It focuses on meeting end-user expectations, enhancing reliability, and ensuring optimal performance under anticipated workloads.

3.2. Building a Performance Engineering Mindset

The first step in adopting a performance engineering approach is to develop a mindset that prioritizes system performance. Everyone in the team, from developers to project managers, should embrace the idea that performance is a critical aspect of the software product and not just a final testing checkpoint.

- Understand the user's perspective: Performance is not just about response times; it also involves smooth navigation, quick loading, consistency, and reliability. Considering performance from the user's perspective can help teams design and deliver a better product.

- Translate performance into requirements: Performance should be expressed in measurable, achievable terms, ideally within your product requirements. These targets will guide design, development, and testing activities.

- Continual performance evaluation: Performance should be continually evaluated throughout each iteration of software development, allowing teams to catch and address issues early.

3.3. Integrating Performance Engineering into Development Lifecycle

Once the right mindset is in place, the next step is to integrate performance engineering practices throughout the development lifecycle.

- Design: Performance engineering starts at the design stage. Consider possibilities like potential traffic volume, simultaneous transactions, data size, etc., while designing the software architecture.

- Development: Code should be written with performance in mind. Regular code reviews can help catch potential performance issues early.

- Testing: In addition to standard unit testing, developers can use profiling tools to measure how well their code performs under stress.

- Deployment: Consider performance during deployment, including factors like hardware sizing and configuration settings.

3.4. Tools and Techniques for Performance Engineering

JMeter, thanks to its robustness and versatility, is an excellent tool to jumpstart your journey into performance engineering. In addition to JMeter, several other tools and technologies can assist:

- Profiling tools: Tools like JProfiler, YourKit, and VisualVM can help optimize code during development.

- APM tools: Application Performance Management (APM) tools like Dynatrace, New Relic, and AppDynamics provide insight into the performance of deployed applications.

- Log analysis tools: Tools like Logstash and Graylog can help analyze logs to identify patterns, errors, or anomalies affecting performance.

3.5. Training and Development

Finally, shifting to a performance engineering paradigm requires ongoing learning and development. Teams should be trained on the core concepts of performance engineering and its integration with lean and agile methodologies. Additionally, investing in professional development in areas like APM tools, cloud computing, and big data can equip your team with the skills needed for advanced performance engineering.

With the shift from load testing to performance engineering, organizations are recognizing that system performance is not merely a desirable feature but a core product requirement. By replacing the traditional, reactive approach with a proactive, holistic focus on efficiency, reliability, and end-user satisfaction, we are seeing a paradigm shift that is strengthening software products and shaping industry standards. With tools like JMeter, embracing performance engineering has never been more attainable. This transformation, both in tools and mindset, is leading us to the pinnacle of system performance.

Chapter 4. Mastering Essential Aspects of Load Testing

Understanding the fundamentals of load testing is instrumental in optimizing software performance. This chapter aims to furnish you with the essential advanced tools and techniques of load testing, including planning and designing tests, understanding performance metrics, handling concurrent users, and utilizing scripting for advanced scenarios.

4.1. Load Testing Planning and Design

Defining clear goals is the first step towards planning a comprehensive load test. You must identify the critical business transactions to be tested, estimate the system's expected workload, and clarify the success criteria. Spelling out the target response time, error rate, and the maximum number of users that need to be supported can significantly streamline the testing process.

The design phase includes scripting and developing test data. Scripters must be well-versed with the application's functionalities and potential bottlenecks.

4.2. Performance Metrics

Understanding performance metrics is key to interpreting the results of load tests. Essential performance metrics include response time, throughput, and resource utilization.

The response time metric measures how long it takes for the server to respond to a user request. This will give you the clearest indication of your application's performance from an end-user's perspective.

Throughput measures the number of requests that can be handled by the server within a specific time frame. It helps in understanding the load an application can bear before performance starts to dip.

Resource utilization concerns itself with how the system's resources, such as CPU, memory, disk I/O, and network I/O, are used under the load.

4.3. Handling Concurrent Users

An application must be able to efficiently handle multiple users concurrently. This involves designing and implementing a user-arrival model, predicting the number of concurrent users, and properly calibrating virtual users in JMeter.

The user-arrival model allows us to anticipate the flow and timing of user requests. Predicting the peak number of concurrent users will help in designing load test scenarios.

4.4. Advanced Scripting

Advanced scripting techniques like parameterization, correlation, and assertions can enhance the realism and effectiveness of load tests.

Parameterization ensures the uniqueness of input data for different virtual users. It is essential whenever multiple concurrent users are simulated to make a load test as realistic as possible.

Correlation, whereas, is about handling dynamic server responses. A server may generate a different response for each user or session, which is crucial to capture and use in subsequent requests.

Assertions are JMeter's way of defining the success criteria of a request. You can inspect a server's response to ensure it matches the expected value, ensuring that the server is both alive and delivering accurate content under load.

By mastering these concepts, you will have the tools to design and execute effective load tests—providing the data you need to optimize performance and reliability. The knowledge of planning, key metrics, handling concurrency, and scripting will elevate your software testing from simple load to advanced performance testing. With diligent practice and refinement, these essential aspects will ensure your software stands up under pressure, improves user satisfaction, and ultimately triumphs in the competitive digital landscape.

Chapter 5. Demystifying Advanced JMeter Concepts and Strategies

Let's delve into the myriad advanced concepts and strategies that JMeter has to offer. Here, we aim to clarify these advanced aspects to enable you to shift your focus from basic load testing to comprehensive performance engineering.

5.1. Understanding Advanced Load Testing

In load testing, our primary objective is to understand how a system behaves under specific loads. With Advanced JMeter strategies, one can simulate various realities, ranging from a sudden spell of elevated traffic, to a gradual accumulation of users over a stretch of time.

For instance, the Thread Group element in JMeter provides options for setting Number of Threads (users), Ramp-up period and Loop Count. These can be fine-tuned to mirror varying user behavior patterns or traffic spikes. There's also the option of a Scheduler, wherein one can define start and end times, carrying out testing as per pre-set schedules.

5.2. Tests with Dynamic Data

A common real-world situation is different users using different data. In JMeter, this is simulated via CSV Data Set Config. Here, data for each user/thread comes from a separate, specified row from the CSV file. With this, each user can be structured to log in with a unique username/password. Importantly, the order in which these credentials are read can also be controlled.

To harness this effectively, one must first create a CSV file with the requisite data. Subsequently, in the CSV Data Set Config, we input the file's location, variable names, and order of reading data.

```
|===
|Column 1|Column 2|Column 3
|Username|Password|Order
|[username1]|[password1]|1
|[username2]|[password2]|2
|===
```

5.3. Introducing Assertions in JMeter

Assertions are crucial for validating your software's response under tests. They allow us to check if a server response contains (or lacks) precise information. JMeter presents numerous types of assertions to cater to an array of use-cases. However, they must be used judiciously, as each assertion evaluates every sample, thereby consuming resources.

1. Response Assertion: This type helps verify that your server under test returns the expected results.

2. Duration Assertion: It ensures the server's response is received within a designated time frame.

3. Size Assertion: This type checks the size of the server's response.

5.4. Correlation in Load Testing

While dealing with dynamic values sent from the server that change with each user session or each new access, correlation becomes significant. These include session IDs, field values, or confirmation codes. Correlation is the process of capturing and storing these dynamic values, then reusing them in subsequent requests.

The basic steps to implement correlation in JMeter include:

1. Identify the dynamic values that require correlation.

2. Insert an Extractor (Regular Expression Extractor, CSS Selector Extractor, or others) to the required HTTP Request sampler to capture the dynamic value.

3. Store the captured value in a variable.

4. Reference this variable where this value needs to be used.

With these steps, you can emulate a realistic user interaction where dynamic values from the server are validated and utilized in subsequent requests.

5.5. Incorporating Listeners

Listeners process the test results in JMeter. From viewing the results as simple data tables to more visual summaries, graphs, or charts, listeners provide a varied range of report generation.

Notable listeners include:

1. View Results Tree: Displays the response message for every request in the tree structure.

2. Summary Report: Provides a statistical summary of the test scenario results.

3. Graph Results: Offers a visual representation of how the server

behaves under different load conditions.

However, it is crucial to remember that listeners consume more memory. It is wise to restrict their usage during high load tests or to judiciously choose the 'Only save data on error' or 'Don't save samples' options.

This detailed exploration of advanced JMeter concepts offers an invaluable treasure trove of strategies to effectively map real world situations, and ensure that your systems are robust and user-friendly. While JMeter's GUI might seem complex initially, remember that mastering this tool will empower you to design efficient systems capable of serving variable users' needs under a vast array of conditions. Happy Performance Engineering!

Chapter 6. Scripting in JMeter: A Beginner's Guide

Before we venture into the world of scripting capabilities in JMeter, it's essential to lay some groundwork. Apache JMeter is an open-source desktop application designed to load test functional behavior and evaluate performance. However, when basic strategies are not enough, we turn to scripting in JMeter for advanced performance testing.

6.1. Understanding JMeter Scripting

Scripting in JMeter refers to the ability to handle more complex scenarios than the regular point-and-click style. It relates to the use of plugins or built-in components that use scripts written in Java, Beanshell, Groovy, or JavaScript to extend functionality.

Chapter 7. Exploring JMeter's Scripting Languages

JMeter's scripting languages play a key role in its versatility. Let's dig into each of them.

7.1. Java

Java is used primarily for writing JMeter Plugins. To use Java you should know about Java programming, JMeter API, and how JMeter works. The learning curve isn't gentle, but Java offers the best performance and can create new JMeter components.

7.2. Beanshell

Beanshell is a small, free, embeddable Java source interpreter with object scripting language features. In JMeter, it's useful for creating complex data modification logic inside scripts, accessing and updating variables, adding conditional pauses, etc. However, it is slower than Java and Groovy.

7.3. Groovy

Groovy is another popular scripting language for JMeter due to its excellent performance and seamless integration with Java. It's a dynamic language with features similar to Python, Ruby, Perl, and Smalltalk. Groovy excels in its scripting for data types manipulation.

7.4. JavaScript

While JavaScript is available in JMeter for scripting, it is the slowest compared to other languages and does not directly support JMeter

Variables.

Chapter 8. Starting with Beanshell Scripting

Beanshell is a good starting point because it's very similar to Java, allowing almost any valid Java code to be run as it is. Furthermore, it exposes additional functionalities to make scripting easier and faster.

8.1. Beanshell Sampler

The Beanshell Sampler enables the creation of a 'sample' by scripting in Beanshell. Let's consider a simple example of a BeanShell sampler that sets a JMeter variable named 'myVar' with a string value 'hello, world'.

```
vars.put("myVar","hello, world!");
```

Here, 'vars' is a Beanshell instance representing JMeter's variables. The method 'put' adds a variable or changes an existing variable's value.

Similarly, to get a variable's value, 'get' method is used.

```
String myVar = vars.get("myVar");
```

8.2. Beanshell PreProcessor

Beanshell PreProcessor executes the script before each sampler in the same scope. A simple use case could be to set a variable value that could be used by the following samplers.

```
vars.put("currentTime",
String.valueOf(System.currentTimeMillis()));
```

This script adds a variable 'currentTime' with the current timestamp as its value.

8.3. Beanshell Assertion

Beanshell Assertion evaluates and validates the response using a script. For example, you can check if the response code is not '200'.

```
String responseCode = prev.getResponseCode();
if(!"200".equals(responseCode)){
    Failure = true;
    FailureMessage = "Invalid response code: " +
responseCode;
}
```

In this script, 'prev' represents the previous sampler's result, 'Failure' signals assertion failure, and 'FailureMessage' sets the failure message.

While this is only the tip of the iceberg, it sheds some light on how you can tap into scripting to modulate JMeter's functionality as per your needs. Next, we'll take a look at Groovy, but remember, no matter how daunting the scripting adventure may seem, each step brings you closer to mastering JMeter and, subsequently, the realm of performance engineering.

Chapter 9. Essential JMeter Elements: Objects, Test Plan, and More

The JMeter landscape is populated by various elements, each possessing a unique functionality, playing an instrumental role in devising effective load tests. It is quintessential to understand how to use these elements in the right way and at the right place. So let's assimilate ourselves with some essential JMeter components.

9.1. Thread Groups

A Thread Group is the starting point of any test plan and acts as the base unit of execution in Apache JMeter. Each Thread Group can be considered a separate virtual user configuring the number of users, ramp up period, and number of iterations. More than one Thread Groups can be used in a test plan depending on the scenario.

```
----
Thread Group Properties
|Property|Description|
|Number of Threads|Number of users to simulate|
|Ramp-Up Period (seconds)|Time taken to start all
threads|
|Loop Count|Number of iterations for user|
----
```

The Ramp-Up period is vital; setting too small a time might cause a sudden rush of users, effectively creating a 'Distributed Denial of Service' (DDoS) effect on your system, while a too elevated setting might make it too slow to generate significant traffic. The optimal

Ramp-Up period needs to be calibrated according to your specific situation.

9.2. Samplers

Samplers let JMeter send a specific type of request (like HTTP, FTP) to the server. JMeter facilitates myriad types of samplers, each with customizable configurations catering to your needs, whether requiring an HTTP request or a Database request. Here are some commonly used Samplers.

```
----
Sampler Types
|Sampler|Description|
|HTTP Request|Used to send HTTP/HTTPS requests|
|FTP Request|Used for sending FTP requests|
|JDBC Request|Used to send SQL to a database|
|Java Request|Used to call a static Java class method|
----
```

9.3. Logic Controllers

Logic Controllers decide the order of processing of Samplers in a thread, paving the way for more complex test scenarios beyond independent sequence execution. With different varieties of Logic Controllers, some common ones include Simple Controller (executes children sequentially), Loop Controller (controls how often its children are run), and If Controller (executes children based on a condition).

9.4. Listener Elements

Listeners are pivotal in providing an interface to access and view results of your test execution. JMeter harbors several listeners, each presenting data in a unique perspective. Notable ones include View Results Tree, Aggregate Report, and Graph Results.

```
----
Listener Types
|Listener|Description|
|View Results Tree|Provides detailed request/responses|
|Aggregate Report|Provides table columns of metric data|
|Graph Results|Displays a simple graph of requests|
----
```

Remember to use listeners judiciously because they consume considerable memory and can affect JMeter's performance on weaker hardware configurations.

9.5. Assertions

Assertions in JMeter enable you to verify a request meets certain conditions. This verification can encompass text, size, xml, xpath, and many more. They act as the validation checkpoints to reassure that our system behaves as expected.

```
----
Assertion Types
|Assertion|Description|
|Response Assertion|Checks whether a text/string exists
or not in the server's response|
|Duration Assertion|Verifies the server's response
within a specified amount of time|
|Size Assertion|Checks the size of the server's
response|
|XML Assertion|Verifies the format of the XML response|
```

9.6. Config Elements

Config elements provide customizable configurations for Samplers and other elements. They can adjust settings ranging from user-defined variables, HTTP request defaults, to LDAP and TCP configurations. They function like global attributes which are accessible by all samplers within the scope.

9.7. Test Plan

Finally, the Test Plan encapsulates all of these components. It organizes your testing strategy by bringing together thread groups, samplers, listeners, assertions under one umbrella. From simple single-page testing to complex stress tests simulating thousands of users, the Test Plan is where everything comes together.

```
----

Basic hierarchy of a Test Plan
[Test Plan] -> [Thread Group] -> [Samplers/Controllers]
-> [Listeners/Assertions]
----
```

Understanding these fundamental pieces is a prerequisite before diving deeper into JMeter's extensive capabilities. Remember, tailoring these elements to your unique circumstances is an art in itself and forms the backbone of effective performance engineering.

In the next chapter, we will delve into the practical applications of JMeter, exposing the real potential of these elements, all configured for your performance queries. But for now, keep exploring, keep experimenting.

Chapter 10. Performance Engineering Essentials: Real-World Techniques and Tips

Performance engineering is an interdisciplinary, full-cycle approach aimed at improving the system's performance and behavior throughout its lifecycle to match the defined non-functional requirements such as response time, latency, resource utilization, throughput, and so forth. It is carried out by an array of techniques which we shall discuss in this chapter.

10.1. Understanding the Performance Lifecycle

Performance engineering encompasses not just one stage, but the entire system development lifecycle. The performance lifecycle has the following stages:

1. Requirement Gathering: Define performance goals. Collect and analyze data.

2. Design: Establish a performance model and performance test plan, selecting a suitable architecture and technology stack that can meet performance requirements.

3. Implementation: Develop and execute the performance test as per the test plan. Identify system constraints, bottlenecks.

4. Analysis & Tuning: Identify the root cause of performance issues, rectify them, and retest. Use results to tune system and enhance performance.

5. Monitor Production: Continuously monitor system in production, use feedback to continuously optimize system performance.

Continue iterating this lifecycle, continuously refining and optimizing your system to ensure high-level performance.

10.2. Identifying Potential Bottlenecks

To achieve peak performance, you need to identify the bottlenecks in your system. Bottlenecks are constraints or choke points that limit the throughput and reduce the performance or efficiency. They could be CPU usage, network bandwidth, disk speed, memory, etc.

Identifying these requires comprehensive monitoring of your system, proactive diagnostic activities, and performance testing. Tools like `ps`, `top`, `vmstat`, `iostat`, `netstat`, can give insights about the bottlenecks.

10.3. The Importance of Load Testing

Load testing is an essential aspect of performance engineering. It involves subjecting your system to a series of user requests mimicking real-world conditions to understand how your system performs under various loads.

JMeter excels in this area. It is an open-source software, designed to load test functional behavior and measure the performance. JMeter allows you to simulate network traffic and test application infrastructure under different load types.

10.4. Techniques for Effective Performance Tuning

Performance tuning is the process of optimizing the performance of an IT system, network, or application and improving the speed and efficiency. Some of the common tuning techniques include:

1. Hardware Tuning: Incorporating faster processors, adding more memory, or using faster disk drives.

2. Software Tuning: Adjusting software parameters, updating or modifying software features to improve performance.

3. Network Tuning: Optimizing network traffic by rearranging network routes.

10.5. Real-world Techniques and Tips

Now that we understood the foundation concepts let's learn some real-world techniques.

- Estimating Traffic: Use data like Google Analytics to understand your peak internet traffic times.

- Regular Monitoring and Auditing: Regular system monitoring helps in proactive identification of system performance issues.

- Automate: Automating processes such as builds, testing, and deployments help maintain consistency and cause less variation.

- Continuous Integration/Delivery: Adopt CI/CD pipelines to automatically test your code and incorporate changes quickly.

- Adopt Microservices: Microservices can help to independently and quickly deploy and scale services based on demand.

- Use CDN: Content Delivery Networks (CDN) use geographical proximity as a criterion for delivering Web content rapidly.

- Load Balancing: Distributes network traffic across multiple servers, ensuring no single server bears too heavy a load.

It's crucial to integrate performance engineering in the entirety of software lifecycle. This enables teams to observe and address performance issues at early stages, resulting in cost savings and efficient systems. Next, let's delve into the usage of JMeter from the point of view of performance engineering.

Chapter 11. Using JMeter to Simulate Real-World Scenarios

First, let's understand what JMeter is. JMeter, an open-source software, is a Java application designed to load test functional behavior and measure performance. It was originally developed for testing Web Applications but has since expanded to other test functions.

11.1. Why Simulation of Real-World Scenarios

Software needs to function within a variable set of conditions. It's essential to know how your application will perform under different circumstances before it's live. This is where JMeter can play a vital role. It helps to simulate real-world usage scenarios to gauge how the application will behave under different loads.

11.2. Steps to Use JMeter for Simulating Real-World Scenarios

Let's look at the steps to use JMeter to simulate real-world scenarios.

1. Install and configure Apache JMeter: Download the latest version of JMeter, unpack the distribution archive and set the appropriate JVM options.

2. Design the Test Plan: A test plan describes the steps JMeter will execute when run. After launching JMeter, click on `File > New`. A test plan can consist of one thread group, controller, samplers,

listeners, timers, assertions, and configuration elements.

3. Add Users (Thread Group): Thread Group denotes concurrent users that you will be simulating. It contains settings for the number of threads, ramp-up period, and number of iterations.

4. Add Samplers: Samplers allow JMeter to send requests to a server. It simulates user requests for a web page from the target server.

5. Add Listeners: These enable you to view the results of samplers in a variety of formats.

6. Run the Test Plan: Click Run from the top menu to commence the test plan.

11.3. Implementing Variable User Loads

The concept of variable user load is key while setting up simulated real-world scenarios. It involves setting up JMeter to simulate different user loads at different times.

1. Use 'Ultimate Thread Group': The Ultimate Thread Group provides a more flexible and controllable load simulation. We define different stages of load, each having its own duration, threads, and delay.

2. Use 'Arrivals Thread Group': For simulating real-world user behavior, the 'Arrivals Thread Group' provides an exceptional approach by generating thread arrivals set by the user rate rather than by the traditional concurrent threads parameter.

11.4. Simulating User Behavior

When attempting to simulate real-world scenarios, it's essential to mimic specific user behaviors, not just load. This involves navigation paths, think/wait times, different interactions, etc.

1. Use Logic Controllers: Logic controllers control the order of processing of samplers. Using these, you can create sequences of events to simulate user path flows in an application.

2. Use Timers: To simulate user wait or thinking time we use timers. Different types of timers help to control the delay between the execution of requests.

3. Use Parameterized Requests: Different users might interact with your application differently. For instance, they might provide different input data. To simulate this, JMeter uses parameterization using CSV Data Set Config.

11.5. Examining the Results

Finally, we need to examine the test result data to evaluate application performance.

1. Aggregate Report: This listener provides a table row for each sampler in your test, showcasing overall statistics about the performance.

2. View Results Tree: This listener provides a tree view of all sample responses, allowing you to inspect each sampler's response data in detail.

3. Graph Results: This listener provides a simple visual representation of the performance of your test.

Through this detailed journey into simulating real-world scenarios with JMeter, we've extensively covered everything from why these simulations are important, setting up variable user loads, mimicking user behavior, and finally examining the results. Implementing these strategies and using JMeter effectively, you can ensure your software can withstand the multiple, variable conditions it might encounter once live.

Chapter 12. Moving Beyond the Basics: Advanced JMeter Scenarios

Introducing the world of advanced JMeter operations, it is important for us to reassert the key strength of this robust tool—its flexibility and adaptability. Complex testing scenarios often involve the synchronous execution of multiple scripts, correlation of dynamic values, parameterization, randomization, and functions. Thus, JMeter's prowess lies in its extensive functionality that needs to be mastered to excel in complex load testing scenarios.

12.1. Understanding Synchronous Execution of Multiple Scripts

Performing concurrent execution of multiple JMeter scripts can simulate pressurizing conditions on the application under test. Fortunately, JMeter provides an effective method to execute multiple scripts concurrently.

To concurrently run multiple scripts, we store all JMeter scripts (.jmx files) that need to be executed in one folder. Subsequently, we run a simple Shell script (for Unix-based systems) or Batch script (for Windows) to execute all .jmx files. Here is an example of a Unix-based Shell script for this purpose:

```
#!/bin/bash
for f in /path/to/scripts/*.jmx
do
    ./jmeter -n -t $f -l ${f%.jmx}.jtl
done
```

The -n and -t options in the script are for non-GUI mode and test file execution, respectively. Essentially, this script picks each .jmx file one by one and runs them in a new JMeter instance. The output of each script is stored in a .jtl file.

12.2. Handling Task Correlation

Our next topic of interest, task correlation, is a frequently occurring element in performance testing. In real-world scenarios, we often deal with applications that generate unique user-specific values upon interacting with the server. These are dynamic parameters that correlate different requests and responses.

JMeter provides powerful post-processors for correlation purposes that allow extracting these dynamic values. Let's work with a Regular Expression Extractor as an example. While it may be superseded by the newer Boundary Extractor, its understanding is beneficial.

Suppose we have a response with "userId": "12345", and we need to correlate the userId.

1. Right-click on the Sampler that returns the response

2. Navigate to Add → Post Processors → Regular Expression Extractor

3. Set the following fields:

   ◦ Reference Name: USER_ID

   ◦ Regular Expression: "userId": "(.+?)"

   ◦ Template: 1

By setting these values, any upstream requests can utilize this userId by referring to ${USER_ID} in their request body/path/parameters.

12.3. Parameterization to Simulate Real-World Scenarios

Parameterization, simply put, implies not hard-coding data. Instead, we use varying user-defined values. This is vitally important to prevent caching from impacting the performance statistics. Parameterization is easily achievable in JMeter using the CSV Data Set Config.

To use this, first, we set up a CSV file with different data sets. Next, follow the steps:

1. Add the CSV Data Set Config to your Test Plan (Right-click on Test Plan → Add → Config Element → CSV Data Set Config)

2. Input the following details:

   ◦ Filename: (Full path of your CSV file)

   ◦ Variable Names: (Comma-separated names to represent each column in CSV)

Remember, the CSV Data Set Config should be a sibling or parent of the Sampler that will use the variable names.

Further, to randomize the selection of data from CSV or to pick data sequentially, alter the `Sharing Mode` in the CSV Data Set config.

12.4. Functions and Their Importance

Functions in JMeter are special values that can process input and return values. They are extremely helpful for handling dynamic data and can range from simple mathematical calculations to more complex tasks such as file manipulation, date formatting, and others.

For instance, to generate a random number in a certain range (say between 1 and 100), we can use the Random function like so: ${Random(1,100)}. This will produce a random number between 1 and 100 each time the function is called.

12.5. Conclusion

In the voyage of mastering JMeter, incorporating these advanced concepts is a necessary step. These methodologies are not just theories but foundational skills that will enable you to tackle real-world testing challenges head-on. Despite their complex nature, a gradual and patient exploration into JMeter's functionalities will recompense you with an invaluable skill set, bringing you closer to achieving the pinnacle of performance engineering.

Chapter 13. A Peek Into the Future: Industry Trends in Performance Engineering

The world is changing in unprecedented ways, and the realm of performance engineering is no exception. As we venture into the future, several trends are set to shape this landscape that are driven by the rapid advancements in technology and the constant pursuit of optimal performance. Let's embark on a journey to explore these trends in detail.

13.1. The Surge of AI and Machine Learning

Artificial Intelligence (AI) and Machine Learning (ML) are transforming how performance engineering is done by automating processes and providing valuable insights to create more efficient systems. AI and ML algorithms can be used to analyse enormous volumes of performance data, identify bottlenecks, predict system failures, and recommend improvements. This not only enhances the efficiency of the system but also allows the team to focus on more complex aspects that cannot be automated. In the future, we can expect AI and ML to become integral to performance engineering, marking a shift towards proactive, predictive, and preventative measures, leading to greatly improved performance.

13.2. Rise in Cloud-Based Performance Testing

The adoption of cloud-based solutions for performance testing is picking up pace. One key factor contributing to this trend is the scalability offered by cloud platforms. Companies can easily adjust the size and power of their testing environment depending on the project needs, ensuring they don't overspend on infrastructure. Moreover, cloud-based testing can simulate diverse geographical locations and network conditions, providing a more complete understanding of application performance. The future will likely see more testing tools and platforms being cloud-native, offering integrated services to streamline the performance testing process.

13.3. Emergence of Performance Monitoring as a Service

Performance Monitoring as a Service (PMaaS) is a relatively new trend. It is a software delivery model where a third-party provider hosts and manages performance monitoring solutions, delivering them to users over the internet. As systems become more complex and the need for continuous monitoring increases, more companies will likely turn to PMaaS for convenience and efficiency. PMaaS providers will need to refine and expand their offerings to keep up with the increasing demands, providing more thorough and nuanced insights into system performance.

13.4. The Role of IoT in Performance Engineering

With the internet of things (IoT) revolutionizing how devices interact with each other, we can't overlook its impact on performance engineering. IoT systems generate vast amounts of data, which if harnessed, can provide valuable insights for performance tuning. Also, the inherent distributed nature of IoT systems necessitates special performance considerations. As the ubiquity of IoT devices increases, performance engineers will need to redefine their strategies to ensure smooth and effective operation.

13.5. Real-User Monitoring for Performance Insights

Real-User Monitoring (RUM) tracks and analyses user experiences in real-time, offering live insights into system performance from the user's perspective. Instead of relying on scripted scenarios in synthetic monitoring, RUM offers a more authentic account of performance, including details like load time, transaction paths, and user behaviour patterns. Thus, it becomes crucial for informed decision-making in performance optimization. As user experience becomes a top priority, RUM's future role in performance engineering will likely be even more significant.

13.6. Shift towards Performance Engineering Strategies over Load and Stress Testing

Until recently, load and stress testing were the primary methods for assessing system performance. However, a noticeable trend is the shift towards holistic performance engineering strategies. Performance engineering places an emphasis on the entire lifecycle of a system, requiring a more comprehensive approach to achieve peak performance. This trend reflects a growing understanding that the performance of an IT system isn't simply a technical aspect, but a critical business factor affecting the bottom line and customer satisfaction.

13.7. Containerization and Microservices Architecture

The future of performance engineering will be significantly influenced by architectural patterns like containerization and microservices. These practices make systems more modular and easy to manage, but they also introduce new performance considerations. For each microservice or container, performance engineers will need to individually evaluate and tune performance parameters. This development is likely to spur new tools and methodologies for performance testing in containerized environments and could redefine the standards for system efficiency.

In conclusion, the future of performance engineering will be shaped by a myriad of technological trends and evolving user demands. At its heart will be a commitment to provide seamless user experiences, more robust systems, and efficient performance capabilities. By following these trends closely, organizations can be well prepared to navigate the future of performance engineering and leverage its benefits to the fullest.